Edward Shippen, Lewis Burd Walker

The Settlement of the Waggoners' Accounts

Relating to General Braddock's Expedition Towards Fort Du Quesne

Edward Shippen, Lewis Burd Walker

The Settlement of the Waggoners' Accounts
Relating to General Braddock's Expedition Towards Fort Du Quesne

ISBN/EAN: 9783337329440

Printed in Europe, USA, Canada, Australia, Japan

Cover: Foto ©ninafisch / pixelio.de

More available books at **www.hansebooks.com**

The Burd Papers.

THE SETTLEMENT

OF THE

WAGGONERS' ACCOUNTS RELATING

TO

GENERAL BRADDOCK'S EXPEDITION

TOWARDS

FORT DU QUESNE

BY

EDWARD SHIPPEN, ET AL.,

COMMISSIONERS.

EDITED BY

LEWIS BURD WALKER.

1899.

Seventy copies of this book have been printed, each signed and numbered. This is number 52.

PREFACE.

On January 31st, 1756, Governor Robert Hunter Morris appointed and commissioned Edward Shippen, Samuel Morris, Alexander Stedman and Samuel McCall, Jr., to "audit, liquidate and settle" the accounts of the owners of all Wagons, Teams and Horses hired or destroyed in the expedition of General Braddock against Fort Du Quesne. This commission is printed in the First Series of Pennsylvania Archives, Volume II, Page 598.

The following is endorsed as the account settled by the above named four gentlemen ; it is, however, entirely in the handwriting of Edward Shippen.

It is believed that this account, printed from the original, in the possession of the editor, is of sufficient interest to students of American History to warrant its publication.

THE

WAGGONERS' ACCOUNTS.

April 30   ABRAHAM FERREE, DR.

To cash advanced	5	5	0
To 3 pcs 8-8 pd him by Mr. Scot . .	1	2	6
To 19 days allowed on ye death of one horse at 2-6 . - . . .	4	17	6
Balance	115	6	8
	£126	11	8

CR.

By appraisement of waggon and horses .	85	10	0
By 51 days from Conestogo Creek to ye 9th July, day of battle, at 15s .	38	5	
By 10 bushels oats from hence, at 20d		16	8
By 10 nights hay for 4 horses . .		10	0
Drivers' service, 10 days to Wills Creek	1	5	
By 5 days exp's driver back to Lancaster		5	
	126	11	8

JOHN HOUSTON, DR.

April 30, 1755.

To cash paid by B. F.	.	5	5	
To do paid by Mr. Scott . .	..	1	2	6
To one month hire of a horse,	30			
days, 2s	.	3	0	0
Balance	.	83	4	2
		£ 92	11	8

CR.

By waggon team and horses . .	.	51	10	0
By 51 days from day of battle at 15	.	38	5	
By travelling expenses up . .	.	2	11	8
By 5 days expenses back to Lancaster				
for ye waggoner			5	
		92	11	8

ISAIAH CUSHMAN, DR.

To cash pd by B. F.	.	5	5	
To do pd him by Mr. Scot, 3 ps 8	.	1	2	6
To do pd by Mr. M'Cloud, 2 ps 8	.		15	
Balance	.	97	2	2
		104	4	8

CR.

By waggon team and horses, 51 days	.	63	0	0
By 51 days at 15s	.	38	5	
By travelling exps. up . . .	.	2	11	8
By 8 days expenses waggoner back	.		8	0
		104	4	8

BENJAMIN PRICE, DR.

To cash of Mr. Benjamin Franklin	.	7	0	0
To do paid by Mr. Work . .	.		15	
Balance	.	109	17	5
Transferred to page . . .	.	117	12	4

CR.

By expenses travelling up and down .	4	4	
By 27 days for 10 horses at 2d . .	27	0	0
By 23 days, 8 horses	18	8	0
By 7 days with 7 horses . . .	4	18	0
By 26 days with 7 horses . . .	18	4	0
By 3 horses at £9 lost . . .	27	0	0
By 7 horses sold in Philada. 40s . .	14	0	0
By 47 days at driver at 2d . .	3	18	4
	£117	12	4

PETER LOCK, DR.

To cash pd by B. F.	5	5	0
To ditto pd by Mr. Scott . . .	1	2	6
Balance	70	14	2
	77	1	8
By waggon team	36	0	0
By 50 days from Cumberland to ye day of battle at 150	38	5	0
By travelling expenses up . . .	2	11	8
By 5 days expenses back . . .	0	5	0
	77	1	8

JOHN OVERHOLSTER, Dr.

To cash pd by B. F.	5	5	0
To Do pd by Mr. Scott . . .	1	2	6
To Do one horse returned	3	10	0
Bal	58	4	2
	68	1	8

CR.

By waggon and team	27	0	0
By 51 days to ye field of battle at 15s per diem	38	5	0
By travelling expenses to Fort Cumberland	2	11	8
By 5 days expenses back . . .		5	0
	68	1	8

JOHN CONNAGY, Dr.

To cash paid by B. F.	5	5	0
To ditto paid by Mr. Scott . .	1	2	6
Bal.	86	4	2
	£92	11	8

CR.

By waggon and team	52	0	0
By 50 days at 15s	37	15	0
By travelling expenses to Fort Cumberland	2	11	8
By 5 days expenses back . . .		5	
	92	11	8

JACOB HAINS, DR.

To cash paid by B. F.	5	5	0
To ditto pd by Mr. Scott . . .	1	2	6
Bal.	96	0	5
	102	7	11

CR.

By waggon and team	57	0	0
By 51 days at 15s	38	5	0
By 5 day extraordinary . . .	3	15	0
By travelling expenses . . .	2	11	8
By 11s 3d more.		11	3
By 5 days expenses back . . .		5	0
	102	7	11

DANIEL SCHULZ, Dr.

To cash pd by Mr. Franklin . .	5	5	0
To do pd by Mr. Scot . . .	1	2	6
Bal. :	60	0	5
	66	7	11

CR.

By waggon and team.	.	.	.	24 15	0
By 51 days	.	.	.	38 5	0
By travelling expenses	.	.	2 11	8
By 11s 3d ferriage	.	.	.	11	3
By 5 days expenses back	.	.		5	0

	£66 7 11

MARTIN KENDRICK, DR.

To cash pd by Mr. Franklin	.	.	.	5 5	0
To ditto pd by Mr. Scot	.	.	.	7	6
To ditto pd by Mr. Lake	.	.	.	1 7	0
Bal	.	.	.	.	89 7	5

	96 6 11

CR.

By waggon and team	.	.	.	49 0	0
By 51 days at 15s	.	.	.	38 5	0
By travelling expenses	.	.	2 11	8
By 11s 3d ferriage	.	.	.	11	3
By 5 days expenses back	.	.		5	0
By 57 days (a man's hire) at 2s, always in ye service	.	.	.	.	5 14	0

	96 6 11

SEBASTIAN GRAAF, DR.

To cash pd by Mr. Franklin	.	.	5 5	0
To ditto pd by Mr. Scot	.	.	.	1 2	6
Balance	.	.	.	.	96 0	5

	102 7 11

CR.

By waggon and team	.	.	.	61 0	0
By 51 days	.	.	.	38 5	0
By travelling expenses	.	.	.	3 2	11

	102 7 11

GEORGE SHANK, DR.

To cash paid by Mr. F. . . .	.	5	5	0
To do paid by Mr. Scott . .	.	1	2	6
Balance	.	100	13	5
	£107	0	11

CR.

Ry wagon and team . . .	.	68	0	0
By days only . . .	.	35	13	0
By expenses	.	3	7	11
	107	0	11

FEBRUARY 4.
J. CHRISTIAN HAIR, DR.

To cash pd by Mr. Franklin .	.	3	5	0
To ditto by Mr. Scott . .	.	1	2	6
To 5 days, a horse dying on ye journey .			12	6
Bal. due to Christian Hare .	.	100	12	11
	107	12	11

CR.

By waggon and team . . .	.	66	0	0
By 51 days wagon hire, 15s . .	.	38	5	0
By expenses	.	3	7	11
	107	12	11

JOHN CHRISTY, DR.

To cash paid by Mr. Franklin .	.	5	5	0
To a horse returned . . .	.	11	0	0
Balance	.	69	17	11
	86	2	11

CR.

By waggon and team . . .	.	55	0	0
By 37 days at 15s . . .	.	27	15	0
By expenses	.	3	7	11
	86	2	11

JOHN WELCH, DR.

To cash pd by Mr. Franklin	.	.	5 5 0
To cash pd by Mr. Scott	.	.	1 2 6
Balance	.	.	88 16 3
			£95 3 9

CR.

By waggon and team	.	.	46 0 0
By 51 days waggon at 15s	.	.	38 5 0
By expenses	.	.	3 7 11
By 2 days more waggonage	.	.	1 10 0
By waggon hire to Philada	.	.	6 0 10
			95 3 9

JACOB HARTMAN, DR.

To cash pd by Mr. Franklin	.	.	5 5 0
Balance	.	.	99 7 11
			104 12 11

CR.

By waggon and team	.	.	63 0 0
By 51 days waggon hire	.	.	38 5 0
By expenses	.	.	3 7 11
			104 12 11

MARTIN GROVE, DR.

To cash pd by Mr. Franklin	.	.	5 5 0
To ditto pd by Mr. Scott	.	.	1 2 6
Bal. due to Martin Grove	.	.	83 10 5
			89 17 11

CR.

By waggon and team	.	.	48 10 0
By 51 days wagon hire	.	.	38 5
By expenses	.	.	3 2 11
.			89 17 11

JOHN ROSS, BLUE ROCK, DR.

To cash pd by Mr. Franklin . .	8	8	0
To do pd 2 servts. by Mr. Scott . .	1	10	0
Balance due to Jno. Ross . . .	151	8	8
	£161	6	8

CR.

By 12 horses	81	0	0
By hire of do 50 days at 2s . . .	60	0	0
By travelling expenses; a bushel of oats, per diem, at 2d p bushel . . .	12	0	0
By 2 drivers	8	6	8
	161	6	8

SAMUEL LA FIEVRE, DR.

To cash pd by Mr. Franklin . .	5	5	0
To ditto pd by McCloud . . .	1	2	6
Bal due to Sam'l La Fievre . .	101	15	5
	108	2	11

CR.

By waggon and team lost . . .	66	10	0
By 51 days waggon hire . . .	38	5	0
By expenses	3	7	11
	108	2	11

CALEB SWAINE FOR —— BISHOP.

Due to Caleb Swaine	18	0

CR.

By pasturage of 54 horses . . .	18	0

DANIEL LaFIEVRE, DR.

To cash pd by Mr. Franklin . . .	5	5	0
To do pd by Mr. Scott . . .	1	2	6
To a horse returned, saddle and bridle .	3	0	0
Bal. due to D. L. F.	84	5	5
	£93	12	11

CR.

By waggon and team	52	0	0
By 51 days wagon hire	38	5	
By expenses	3	7	11
	93	12	11

CALEB WORLEY, DR.

To cash pd by Mr. Franklin . .	5	5	0
To do pd by Mr. Scott . . .	1	2	6
Balance due to Caleb Worley . .	88	5	5
	94	12	11

CR.

By waggon and team lost . . .	57	0	0
By waggon hire, &c. . . .	34	5	0
By travelling expenses . . .	3	7	11
	94	12	11

MATTHIAS SLEIGHMAKER, DR.

To cash pd by Mr. Franklin . . .	5	5	0
To do pd by Mr. Scott . . .	1	2	6
Balance due to Mr. Sleighmaker .	95	0	5
	101	7	11

CR.

By waggon & team lost . . .	59	0	0
By 39 days	39	0	0
By travelling expenses . . .	3	7	11
	101	7	11

HENRY BOWER, DR.

To cash pd by B. F.	5	5	0
To do pd by Mr. Scott	1	2	6
Bal. due Mr. Bower	83	5	5
	89	12	11

CR.

By waggon, &c., lost	48	0	0
By 51 days wagon hire	38	5	0
By expenses	3	7	11
	89	12	11

GEBHART BRENHAR, DR.

To cash paid by Mr. Frank	5	5	0
Bal. due to G. Brenhar	98	7	11
	103	12	11

CR.

By waggon and team lost	62	0	0
By 51 days wagon hire	38	5	0
By expenses	3	7	11
	103	12	11

CHARLES RICHARDSON, DR.

To cash pd Mr. Franklin	5	5	0
To do pd by Mr. Scott	1	2	6
To 26 days, ye man dying who drove ye waggon, at 2s	2	12	0
Bal due to C. Richardson	115	13	5
	124	12	11

CR.

By waggon and team lost	83	0	0
By 51 days waggon hire	38	5	0
By expenses	3	7	11
	124	12	11

JACOB WILLHIEM, DR.

To cash pd by Mr. Franklin . . .	5	5	0
To do pd by	1	2	6
Bal. due to J. Willhiem . . .	78	5	5
	£84	12	11

CR.

By waggon and team lost . . .	43	0	0
By 51 days waggon hire . . .	38	5	0
By expenses	3	7	11
	84	12	11

THOMAS SMITH, DR.

To cash pd by Mr. Franklin . .	5	5	0
To do pd by Scott . . .	1	2	6
To do pd by Mr. Lake . . .	1	7	0
Bal. due to Tho Smith . . .	95	12	7
	103	7	1

CR.

By waggon and team lost . . .	55	0	0
By waggon hire and wages . . .	45	4	2
By expenses	3	2	11
	103	7	1

JOHN SMITH, DR.

To cash pd by Mr. Franklin . .	4	4	0
To do pd by Mr. Scott . . .		15	0
Bal. due to John Smith . . .	62	5	11
	67	4	11

CR.

By 6 horses lost	33	10	0
By do hire 51 days at 2s . . .	30	12	0
By expenses	3	2	11
	67	4	11

FEBRUARY YE 5TH.
DANIEL HUFMAN, DR.

To cash pd by Mr. Franklin . . .	5	5	0
To do pd by Mr. M'Cloud . . .		15	0
To a horse returned	6	10	0
Bal. due to D. Hufman . . .	54	15	7
	£67	5	7

CR.

By waggon and team lost . . .	29	0	0
By waggon hire	35	1	0
By expenses	3	4	7
	67	5	7

PETER BRICKER, DR.

To cash pd by Mr. Franklin . .	5	5	0
To do pd by Mr. Scott . . .	1	2	6
To a horse returned	10	0	0
Bal. due P. Bricker	71	15	10
	88	3	4

CR.

By waggon and team lost . . .	53	0	0
By waggon hire	33	13	4
By expenses up only	1	10	0
	88	3	4

BENJAMIN LANDESS, DR.

To cash pd by Mr. B. Franklin . .	5	5	0
To ditto pd by Mr. Scott . . .	1	2	6
Bal. due to B. Landess . . .	78	5	5
	84	12	11

CR.

By waggon and team lost . . .	43	0	0
By waggon hire	38	5	0
By expenses	3	7	11
	84	12	11

MARTIN WHITEMAN, DR.

To cash pd by Mr. Frauklin . . .	5	5	0
To ditto pd by Mr. Lake . . .	1	8	0
To ditto pd by Mr. Scott . . .	1	2	6
Bal. due to M. Whiteman . . .	78	12	5
	£86	7	11

CR.

By waggon and team lost . . .	47	0	0
By 58 days waggon hire at 15s . .	36	0	0
By expenses	3	7	11
	86	7	11

JACOB SNEAVELY, DR.

To cash pd by Mr. Franklin . .	5	5	0
To ditto pd by Mr. Scott . . .	1	7	0
Bal. due to J. Sneavely . . .	96	0	11
	102	12	11

CR.

By waggon and team lost . . .	61	0	0
By waggon hire	38	5	0
By expenses	3	7	11
	102	12	11

JAMES BOYLE, DR.

To cash paid by Mr. Franklin . .	3	10	0
To ditto paid by Mr. Lake . . .	4	1	0
Bal. due to James Boyle . . .	50	15	0
	58	6	0

CR.

By 5 horses lost	40	0	0
By hire for 3 horses 51 days at 2s .	15	6	0
By expenses	3	0	0
	58	5	0

By the above balance 50 15 0
By 63 days wages to ye waggoner at 20d
   per diem 5 5

Bal. due to Jas. Boyle . . £56 0 0

DANIEL LAWREY, DR

To cash pd by Mr. Lake . . . 4 1 0
To 2 horses returned 17 0 0
To cash pd by Capt. Lake . . . 7 8 0
  Bal. due to Dan'l Lawrey . . . 582 16 0

611 5 0

CR.

By 45 horses, at £8 1s, lost . . . 382 10 0
By the hire of sd. 45 horses 43 days, at
  2s. per diem, this was to ye 9th of July 193 10 0
By the hire of 2 horses, from the 9th July
  to the 3rd Sept., 55 days, at 2s . . 11 0 0
By 2 drivers, from 28 May to the 24th
  July is 56 days, at 20d each . . 9 6 8
By 1 driver, from 28 May to the 9th
  August, 71 days, at 20d . . 5 18 4
By expenses for 3 drivers at 60s . . 9 0 0

611 5 0

JACOB MUMMOIA, DR.

To cash pd by Mr. Franklin . . . 5 5 0
To ditto pd by Mr. Scott . . . 1 2 6
To 2 horses returned . . . 22 0 0
To the hire of 2 horses 22 days . . 5 10 0
  Bal. due Jacob Mummoia . . . 53 10 5

87 7 11

CR.

By waggon and team 46 0 0
By waggon hire 38 5 0

By expenses	3	2	11

	£87	7	11

JAMES SIMSON, DR.

To cash pd him by Mr. Franklin . .	4	4	0
To ditto pd him by Mr. Lake . .	19	18	3
To a mare or horse returned . .	8	0	0
Balance due to James Simson . .	63	5	9

	95	8	0

CR.

By the hire of 6 horses 58 days at 2s each	34	16	0
By 6 horses lost at £8	48	0	0
By expenses	3	12	0
By ye driver 108 days at 20d . .	9	0	0

	95	8	0

CHARLES ROAN, DR.

To cash pd him by Mr. Lake . .	22	10	0
To do pd by ditto . .	2	14	0
To do pd by Mr. Scott . . .	1	2	6
To do pd by Mr. Franklin . . .	5	5	0
To bal. due to Charles Roan . .	69	2	5

	100	13	11

CR.

By waggon and team	55	0	0
By waggon hire	35	10	0
By hire, 2 horses 13 days . . .	2	12	0
By do 1 do 42 . . .	4	4	0
By expenses	3	7	11

	100	13	11

WILLIAM ILENRY, DR.

To cash pd by Mr. Franklin . .	5	5	0
To ditto pd by Mr. Lake . . .	9	10	0
To a horse returned	7	0	0
To the hire of 2 horses 15 days . .	3	15	0
Bal due to W. Henry . . .	67	15	5
	£93	5	5

CR.

By waggon and horses lost . . .	50	0	0
By waggon hire	38	5	0
By expenses	3	7	11
By 13 days horse hire	1	12	6
	93	5	5

JACOB ROHRER, DR.

To cash pd by Mr. Franklin . . .	5	5	0
To ditto pd by Mr. Scott . . .	1	2	6
To the hire of a driver, 40 days at 2s 6d .	5	0	0
Bal. due to Jacob Rohrer . . .	77	5	5
	88	12	11

CR.

By waggon and team lost . . .	44	0	0
By waggon hire	38	5	0
By expenses	3	2	11
By the hire of two horses 13 days . .	3	5	0
	88	12	11

VINCENT MYER, DR.

To cash pd by Mr. Franklin . . .	5	5	0
To the waggon	11	0	0
To a horse returned	12	0	0
Bal. due to V. Myer	47	17	11
	76	2	11

CR.

By waggon and team	49	0	0
By the hire of 3 horses fifty days at 2s. 6d., with geers	18	15	0
By expenses	3	7	11
By the waggoner's service, 30 days .	5	0	0
	£76	2	11

JOHN MILLER. DR.

To cash pd by Mr. Franklin . .	5	5	0
To do pd by Mr. Scott . . .	1	2	6
To a horse returned	12	0	0
Bal due to John Miller . . .	88	14	7
	107	2	1

CR.

By wagon and team	54	0	0
By waggon hire	38	5	0
By expenses	3	7	11
By 55 days man and horse at 4s. 2d. .	11	9	2
	107	2	1

JAMES RANKIN, DR.

To cash paid him by Mr. Lake . .	4	8	5
Bal. due to Jas. Rankin . . .	13	18	9
	18	7	2

CR.

By wages due as horsemaster by order of Genl. Shirly	18	7	2

FEBRUARY THE 6 DAY.

JAMES LAWREY, DR.

To cash pd by Mr. Franklin . . .	21	0	0
To ditto pd by Mr. Lake . . .	2	14	0
To one horse returned	10	0	0
Bal. due to James Lawrey . .	372	8	0
	406	2	0

CR.

By 28 horses valued at £10 each .	280	0	0
By hire of 28 horses 42 days at 2s each			
per diem	117	12	0
By the hire of 1 horse 55 days at 2s per			
diem	5	10	0
By expenses and c	3	0	0
	£406	2	0

FREDERICK DREASH, DR.

To cash pd by Mr. Lake . . .	4	1	0
To do pd by Mr. Scott . . .	1	2	6
Balance due to Frederick Dreash .	10	4	0
	15	7	6

CR.

By 41 days as waggon Mr. at 7s 6d .	15	7	6

JAMES KAR, DR.

To cash pd by Mr. Franklin . . .	5	5	0
To ditto pd by Mr. Scott . . .	1	2	6
To ditto pd by Mr. Lake . . .	12	14	0
Balance due to Jas. Kar . . .	88	1	5
	97	2	11

CR.

By waggon and team	54	0	0
By wagon hire	39	15	0
By expenses	3	7	11
	97	2	11

JOHN MOORE, DR.

To cash pd by Mr. Franklin . .	5	5	0
To ditto pd by Mr. Scott . . .	1	2	6
Balance due	71	5	5
	77	12	11

CR.

		£	s.	d.
By waggon and team	.	36	0	0
By hire of ditto	.	38	5	0
By expenses	.	3	7	11
		£77	12	11

THOMAS KITTERA, DR.

		£	s.	d.
To cash pd by Mr. Franklin .	.	5	5	0
To ditto pd by Mr. Scott . .	.	1	2	6
To ditto paid by Mr. Lake . .	.	2	17	2
To a horse returned . .	.	8	0	0
Bal. due to T. Kittera . .	.	82	17	5
		100	2	1

CR.

		£	s.	d.
By waggon and team . . .	.	47	0	0
By hire of ditto	.	38	5	0
By hire man and horse 55 days at 4s 2d per diem	.	11	9	2
By expenses	.	3	7	11
		100	2	1

WILLIAM DOUGLAS, DR.

		£	s.	d.
To cash pd by Mr. Franklin . .	.	5	5	0
To do pd by Mr. Scott . ·	.	1	2	6
To 3 horses returned . .	.	28	0	0
To the waggon returned . .	.	16	0	0
Bal. due to W. Douglas . .	.	79	12	11
		180	0	5

CR.

		£	s	d
By waggon and team		£34	0	0
By hire of ditto		38	5	0
By hire of waggon and 3 horses 55 days at 12s 3d		34	7	6
By expenses		3	7	11
		£130	0	5

THE SAME WILLIAM DOUGLAS, DR.

To cash paid by Mr. Franklin		5	5	0
To do paid by Mr. Scott		1	2	6
To do pd by Mr. Lake		1	7	0
To bal. due to W. Douglas		105	0	1
		112	14	7

CR.

By waggon and team lost		60	0	0
By hire of ditto, &c		49	6	8
By expenses		3	7	11
		112	14	7

JOHN BOGGS, DR.

To cash pd by Mr. Lake		1	7	0
Bal. due to John Boggs		3	9	8
		4	16	8

CR.

By hire & driver		4	16	8

MARTIN CROYDER, DR.

To cash pd by Mr. Franklin		5	5	0
To do pd by Mr. Scott		1	2	6
Bal. due to Martin Croyder		90	5	5
		96	12	11

CR.

By waggon and team lost	.	.	.	55	0	0
By waggon hire	.	.	.	.	38	5	0
By expenses	.	.	.	.	.	3	7	11

£96 12 11

WILLIAM WILKYNS, DR

To cash pd by Mr. Franklin	.	.	4	4	0
To do pd by Mr. Lake	.	.	.	1	7	0
To do pd by Mr. Scott	.	.	.	.	15	0
To a horse returned	.	.	.	6	10	0
Bal. due to W. W.	.	.	.	76	13	0

89 9 0

CR.

By 6 horses lost at £8 10s	.	.	51	0	0
By hire ditto 42 days at 2s	.	.	25	4	0
By ditto of 1 horse 55 days at 2s	.	.	5	10	0
By wages driver 57 days at 20d	-	.	4	15	0
By expenses	.	.	.	.	3	0	0

89 9 0

ANDREW BOGGS, DR.

Due to Andrew Boggs	.	.	.	1	7	6

CR.

By 11 days horse hire 2s 6d .	.	.	1	7	6

JOHN GARBER, DR.

To cash paid by Mr. Franklin	.	.	5	5	0
To do pd by Mr. Lake	.	.	.	1	8	0
To do pd by Scott	.	.	.	1	2	6
Bal. due to A. Boggs (J. Garber?)	.	62	19	11

70 15 5

Cr.

By waggon and team lost . . .	30	10	0
By hire of do	36	17	6
By expenses	3	7	11
	£70	15	5

Emanuel Carpenter, Dr.

To cash of Mr. Franklin . . .	4	4	0
To a horse returned	4	0	0
Bal. due to E. Carp'r . .	62	15	8
	80	19	8

Cr.

By 6 horses lost	44	10	0
By ditto 49 days at 2s . . .	29	8	0
By 49 days wages a man at 20d . .	4	1	8
By expenses	3	0	0
	80	19	8

Josiah Scott, Dr.

To cash pd by Mr. Franklin . .	5	5	0
To do pd by Mr. Scott . . .	1	2	6
To do pd by Mr. Lake . . .	4	1	6
To one grey horse returned . .	14	0	0
Bal. due to Josiah Scott . .	90	3	1
	114	12	1

Cr.

By waggon and team lost . .	61	10	0
By waggon hire	38	5	0
By expenses	3	7	11
By a horse and driver, 55 @ 4s 2d .	11	9	2
	114	12	1

CHRISTIAN WALBONE, OWNER, DR.
Frederick Lander, Driver.

To cash pd by Mr. Franklin	5	5	0
To do paid by Mr. Scott	1	2	6
To ditto paid by Mr. Lake	1	7	0
To 2 horses returned	13	10	0
Bal. due Christian Walbone	82	10	1
	£103	14	7

CR.

By waggon and team lost	44	0	0
By hire of the waggon	38	5	0
By expenses	3	2	11
By 55 days at 6s 7d drivers & horses	8	6	8
	103	14	7

JOHN GALBRAITH, DR.

To cash pd by Mr. Franklin	13	6	0
To cash pd by Mr. Lake	3	12	0
Balance due to Jno. Galbr.	168	11	8
	185	9	8

CR.

By 13 horses lost	117	0	0
By hire ditto 43 days	55	18	0
By hire of driver	3	11	8
By expenses	9	0	0
	185	9	8

RICHARD MAGEE, DR.

To cash paid by Mr. Lake	1	7	0
To do pd by Mr. Scott		15	0
Balance due to R. Magee	52	13	8
	54	15	8

CR.

By 4 horses at £7 15 lost . . .	31	0	0
By hire of ditto	17	4	0
By hire of ye driver	3	11	8
By expenses	3	0	0
	£54	15	8

MICHAEL BAUCHMAN, DR.

Due to Mich. Bauchman . . .	33	0	0

CR.

By waggon hire to Shippensburg . .	3	0	0
By valuation of 2 horses, 3 bridles and 2 saddles	30	0	
	33	0	0

THOMAS MITCHELL, DR., FEBRUARY 7TH.

To cash pd by Mr. Frankiin . .	21	0	0
To a horse returned	10	0	0
To cash paid Reed Mitehell by Mr. Lake	3	2	8
Balance due to Tho. Mitchell . .	380	11	4
	414	14	0

CR.

By 29 horses lost	290	0	0
By hire 29 horses 43 days at 2s . .	124	14	0
	414	14	0

GEORGE LITTLE, DR.

To cash paid by Mr. Frauklin . .	5	5	0
To ditto pd by Mr. Scott . . .	1	2	6
Bal. due to Geo. Little . . .	84	5	5
	90	12	11

CR.

By waggon and team lost	.	.	.	49 0 0
By waggon and horses lost	.	.	.	38 5 0
By expenses .	.	.	.	.	3 7 11

£90 12 11

JAMES COOK, DR.

To cash pd by Mr. Franklin .	.	.	7 0 0
To ditto pd by Mr. Lake	.	.	4 1 6
Bal. due to James Cook	.	.	130 10 2

141 11 8

CR.

By 10 horses	.	.	.	.	90 0 0
By hire ditto 43 days	.	.	.	43 0 0
By driver's hire, 43 days at 20d	.	.	3 11 8
By expenses .	.	.	.	.	5 0 0

141 11 8

BALTAZZAR SPANGLER, DR.

To cash pd by Mr. Franklin	.	.	5 5 0
To do paid by Mr. Cloude	.	.	15 0
To 3 horses .	.	.	.	27 0 0
To Bal due to B. S.	.	.	70 11 0

103 11 0

CR.

By waggon and team lost	.	.	.	44 11 0
By waggon hire .	.	.	.	38 5 0
By hire of 3 horses	.	.	.	16 10 0
By travelling expenses	.	.	.	3 0 0
By driver's hire, 15 days	.	.	.	1 5 0

103 11 0

PHILIP RUDYSELLY, DR.

	£	s	d
To cash pd by Mr. Franklin . .	5	5	0
To ditto pd by Mr. Scott . . .	1	2	6
To a horse returned	14	0	0
To a sorrell horse Philada. . .	10	0	0
Bal. due to P. R.	67	0	5
	£97	7	11

CR.

	£	s	d
By waggon and team	44	0	0
By waggon hire	38	5	0
By expenses	3	2	11
By a horse sold in Philada. . .	2	0	0
	97	7	11

ISAAC BEAR, DR.

	£	s	d
To cash pd by Mr. Franklin . .	5	5	0
To ditto pd by Mr. Scott . . .	1	2	6
Bal due to I. Bear	79	5	5
	85	12	11

CR.

	£	s	d
By waggon and team lost . . .	44	0	0
By waggon hire	38	5	0
By expenses	3	7	11
	85	12	11

JACOB DOWNER, DR.

	£	s	d
To cash pd by Mr. Franklin . .	5	5	0
To ditto pd by Mr. Scott . . .	1	2	0
Bal due to J. Downer . . .	88	12	11
	95	0	5

CR.

By waggon and team lost . . .	50	0	0
By waggon hire	36	0	0
By travel'g exps	3	7	11
By 9 days service with 4 horses . .	5	12	6
	£95	0	5

CHRISTIAN BRINNIMAN, DR.

To cash paid by Mr. Franklin . .	4	4	0
Bal. due to C. B.	15	17	8
	63	1	8

CR.

By 5 horses	31	10	0
By 5 horses, 49 days at 2s . . .	24	10	0
By driver 49 do at 20d . . .	4	1	8
By travelling expenses . . .	3	0	0
	63	1	8

PHILIP UPRIGHT, DR.

To cash paid by Mr. Franklin . .	5	5	0
To ditto pd by Mr. Scott . . .	1	2	6
To do pd by Mr. Lake . . .	1	7	0
Bal. due to P. U.	64	13	5
	72	7	11

CR.

By waggon and team	46	0	0
By waggon hire	20	5	0
By horse hire 22 days 2s 6d . . .	2	15	0
By expenses	3	7	11
	72	7	11

PHILIP CROL, DR.

B. due to P. C.	19	10	0

CR.

By 101 days as assistant waggon master
  at 3s 9d 18 18 9
By expenses 11 3

                             £19 10 0

HANS ADAM LIPPART, DR.

To cash pd by Mr. Franklin . . .   5 5 0
To ditto pd by Mr. Scott . . .   1 2 6
By 2 horses returned 17 0 0
  Balance due to H. A. L. . . . 66 0 5

                             89 7 11

CR.

By waggon and team lost . . . 56 0 0
By waggon hire 88 5 0
By expenses 3 2 11

                             89 7 11

JOHN HOPSON, DR.

To cash pd by Mr. Franklin . . .   5 5 0
  Balance due to Jno. Hopson . . 92 7 11

                             97 12 11

CR.

By waggon and team lost . . . 56 0 0
By waggon hire 38 5 0
By expenses 3 7 11

                             97 12 11

JONH RORA, DR.

To cash pd by Mr. Franklin . . .   5 5 0
  Bal. due 112 7 11

                           117 12 11

CR.

By waggon and team lost	.	.	.	76	0	0
By waggon hire	.	.	.	.	38	5	0
By expenses .	.	.	.	.	3	7	11

£117 12 11

SAMUEL SCOTT, DR.

Due to Samuel Scott 18 0

CR.

By pasturage for 54 horses . . ,   18 0

BARNABAS HUGHES, DR.

To cash pd by Mr. Franklin . . .   5 5 0
To 2 horses hire 14 days . . .   3 10 0
Balance due to B. II. . . . 85 7 11

94 2 11

CR.

By waggon and team 31 10 0
By waggon hire 38 5 0
By expenses 3 7 11

94 2 11

THE SAME BARNABAS HUGHES, DR.

To cash paid by Mr. Scott . . .   11 3
To do paid by Mr. Lake . . . 2 14 0
To do of do 40 7 0
To 2 horses returned : . . . 14 10 0
Bal. due to B. H. . . . 24 3 1

82 5 4

CR.

By 6 horses 43 4 0
By hire of do 29 8 0
By hire of ye driver 6 13 4
By expenses 3 0 0

82 5 4

MICHAEL DAVATAVER, DR.

To cash paid by Mr. Franklin . .	5	5	0
To do pd by Mr. Scott	1	2	6
Bal. due	83	5	5
	£89	12	11

CR.

By waggon and team	48	0	0
By hire of ditto	38	5	0
By expenses	3	7	11
	89	12	11

JOHN HAMBRIGHT, DR.

Due to Jno. Hambright . . .	6	1	4

CR.

By pasturage of 64 horses 1 night .	1	1	4
By a horse	5	0	0
	6	1	4

DANIEL HARMAN, DR.

To cash paid by Mr. Frank . . .	4	4	0
To do pd by Capt. Scott . . .		15	0
To do pd by Mr. Lake . . .	1	7	0
Bal. due to D. H. . . .	66	3	8
	72	9	8

CR.

By 6 horses	36	0	0
By hire for ditto 49 days . .	29	8	0
By hire for ye driver 49 days at 20d .	4	1	8
By expenses	3	0	0
	72	9	8

CONRAD HOLSPALM, DR., FEBY. 9TH.

To cash paid by Mr. Frank . . .	5	5	0
Bal. due to Conrad H. . . .	73	0	0
	£78	5	0

CR.

By waggon and team	37	0	0
By hire of ditto	38	5	0
By expenses	3	0	0
	78	5	0

TOBIAS AMSPOCKER, DR.

To cash paid by Mr. Franklin . .	5	5	0
To cash paid by Scott	1	2	6
To a horse returned	8	10	0
Bal. due to Tobias	63	17	6
	78	15	0

CR.

By waggon and team lost . . .	41	0	0
By waggon hire	34	15	0
By expenses	3	0	0
	78	15	0

JOHN SMITH (OF YORK) DR.

To cash paid by Mr. Franklin . .	5	5	0
Balance	70	17	11
	76	2	11

CR.

By waggon and team lost . . .	34	10	0
By waggon hire	38	5	0
By expenses	3	7	11
	76	2	11

HENRY CLEVER, DR.

To cash pd by Mr. Franklin . . .	5	5	0
Bal. due to H. Clever . . .	72	10	0
	£77	15	0

CR.

By waggon and team lost . . .	39	10	0
By waggon hire	35	5	0
By expenses York . , . .	3	0	0
	77	15	0

CHRISTIAN WALBONE, DR.

To cash pd by Mr. Franklin . . .	5	5	0
Bal. due to C. Walbone . . .	65	7	11
	70	12	11

CR.

By waggon and team	29	0	0
By waggon hire	38	5	0
By expenses	3	7	11
	70	12	11

THE SAME CHRISTIAN WALBONE, DR.

To cash paid by Mr. Franklin . .	5	5	0
Bal. due to C. Walbone . . .	62	2	11
	67	7	11

CR.

By waggon and team	26	0	0
By hire of ditto	38	0	0
By expenses	3	7	11
	67	7	11

The same Christian Walbone, Dr.

To cash pd by Mr. Franklin . . .	5	5	0
Balance due to C. W. . . .	74	17	11
	£80	2	11

Cr.

By waggon and team	38	10	0
By hire of do	38	5	0
By expenses	3	7	11
	80	2	11

Henry Spegat, Dr.

To cash paid by Mr. Franklin . .	5	5	0
	67	15	0
	73	0	0

Cr.

By waggon and team . . .	34	0	0
By hire of ditto	36	0	0
By expenses (York) . . .	3	0	0
	73	0	0

George Ernst Myers, Dr.

To cash paid by Mr. Franklin . .	5	5	0
Bal. due to G. E. Myers . .	63	17	0
	69	2	0

Cr.

By waggon and team	35	10	0
By hire of ditto	30	12	0
By expenses (York) . . .	3	0	0
	69	2	0

BERNARD LAUMAN, DR.

To cash pd by Mr. Franklin	.	.	5	5	0
Balance due to B. L.	.	.	.	69	10	0
			£74	15	0

CR.

By waggon and team lost	.	.	.	29	15	0
By hire of ditto	.	.	.	.	42	0	0
By expenses (York)	.	.	.	.	3	0	0
			74	15	0

FRANCIS WORLEY, DR.

To cash pd by Mr. Franklin	.	.	5	5	0
Balance due to F. W.	.	.	.	58	10	0
			63	15	0

CR.

By Worley (Waggon?) and team .	.	35	10	0
By hire of ditto	.	.	.	.	25	5	0
By expenses (York)	.	.	.	.	3	0	0
			63	15	0

HENRY ANDSMANKS, DR.

To cash pd by Mr. Franklin	.	.	5	5	0
To a horse returned	.	.	.	4	10	0
Bal.	.	.	.	.	.	.	73	5	0
			83	0	0

CR.

By waggon and team	.	.	.	33	10	0
To hire of ditto	.	.	.	.	38	5	0
By expenses (York)	.	.	.	3	0	0
By hire of 2 horses, York	.	.	.	8	5	0
			83	0	0

GEORGE ELEFRITZ, DR.

To cash pd by Mr. Franklin	. .	5	5	0
To a horse returned . . .	.	9	0	0
Balance due to G. E. . .	.	61	10	0
		£75	15	0

CR.

By waggon and team . . .	.	34	10	0
By hire of ditto	.	38	5	0
By expenses (York) . . .	.	3	0	0
		75	15	0

PETER TREAD, DR.

To cash pd by Mr. Tr. . . .	.	5	5	0
Balance due to P. T. . .	.	60	13	0
		65	18	0

CR.

By waggon and team . . .	.	38	10	0
By hire of ditto	.	24	8	0
By expenses	.	3	0	0
		65	18	0

ABRAHAM BEAR, DR.

To cash pd by Mr. F. . . .	.	5	5	0
To ditto pd by Mr. Scott . .	.	1	7	0
To a horse returned . . .	.	16	0	0
Balance due to A. B. . .	.	74	10	11
		97	2	11

CR.

By waggon and team . . .	.	58	0	0
By hire of ditto	.	35	15	0
By expenses	.	3	7	11
		97	2	11

CHRISTOPHER FRY, DR.

To cash pd by Mr. Franklin	.	.	5 5 0
To ditto pd by Mr. Scott	.	.	1 2 6
Bal. due to C. Fry	.	.	95 5 5

£101 12 11

CR.

By waggon and team	.	.	60 0 0
By hire of ditto	.	.	38 5 0
By expenses	.	.	3 7 11

101 12 11

JOHN AMENT, DR.

To cash pd by Mr. Franklin .	.	.	5 5 0
Bal. due to Jno. Ament	.	.	68 18 0

74 3 0

CR.

By waggon and team lost	.	.	34 10 0
By hire of ditto	.	.	36 13 0
By expenses (York)	.	.	3 0 0

74 3 0

THOMAS JERVIS, DR.

Due to Thomas Jervis . . . 12 11 2
CR.
By pasturage of horses at Philada. . 12 11 2

MICHAEL BOWER, DR.

To cash pd by Mr. Franklin .	.	.	5 5 0
To a horse returned	.	.	8 0 0
Bal. due to M. Bower	.	.	76 5 0

89 10 0

CR.

		£	s	d
By waggon and team lost	. . .	40	2	6
By hire of ditto	. . . . .	46	7	6
By expenses	. . . .	3	0	0
		£89	10	0

JACOB WELCHOUER, DR.

		£	s	d
To cash pd by Mr. Franklin	. . .	5	5	0
To a horse returned	. . . .	2	5	0
Bal. due to J. W.	. . . .	68	7	6
		75	17	6

CR.

		£	s	d
By waggon and team lost	. . .	36	10	0
By hire of ditto	. . . . .	36	7	6
By expenses	. . . .	3	0	0
		75	17	6

CHRISTIAN BIXLER, DR.

		£	s	d
To cash pd by Mr. F.	. . . .	5	5	0
Bal due to C. B.	. . . .	70	15	0
		76	0	0

CR.

		£	s	d
By waggon and team	. . . .	34	15	0
By hire of do	. . . . .	38	5	0
By expenses (YORK)	. . . .	3	0	0
		76	0	0

JAMES PATTERSON, DR.

		£	s	d
To cash pd by Mr. Franklin	. . .	5	5	0
To ditto of Mr. Leake	. . . .	4	4	0
To a mare returned	. . .	14	0	0
Bal. due to Jas. Patterson	. . .	85	18	11
		109	7	11

CR.

By waggon and team	56	0	0
By hire of ditto	49	10	0
By expenses	3	7	11
By services of a boy . . .		10	0
	£109	7	11

THOMAS BARTHOLOMEW, DR.

Due to Bartho	6	2	2

CR.

By 32 horses pasturage	6	2	2

JACOB DONER, DR.

To cash paid by Mr. Franklin . .	4	4	0
To do pd by Mr. Scott . . .		15	0
To do paid by Mr. Work . .	1	7	0
To do paid by Mr. Lake . .	1	7	0
Bal.	52	19	0
	60	12	0

CR.

By 6 horses	23	10	0
By driver 78 days at 1s 8d. . .	6	10	0
By expenses	3	0	0
By hire of 46 days ye horses . .	27	12	0
	60	12	0

DAVID STOUT, DR.

To cash pd by Mr. Scott . . .		15	0
To do pd Mr. Work . . .		7	6
Bal. due to D. Stout . . .	56	1	6
	57	4	0

CR.

By 5 horses	29	8	0
By hire ditto	20	6	0
By driver	5	0	0
By expenses	2	10	0
	£57	4	0

JOHN SHULTS, DR.

To cash pd by Mr. Franklin . .	5	5	0
To do pd by Mr. Lake		7	6
Balance due to J. S.	71	15	6
	77	8	0

CR.

By wagon and team	40	10	0
By hire of ditto	33	18	0
By expenses	3	0	0
	77	8	0

HENRY LIPHART, DR.

To cash pd by Mr. Franklin . . .	5	5	0
To do pd by Mr. McCloud . . .		7	6
To a horse returned	7	10	0
Bal.	74	12	6
	87	15	0

CR.

By waggon and team	39	0	0
By waggon hire	41	5	0
By expenses (York)	3	0	0
By a horse to Philada. 35 days at 2s. 6d.	4	10	0
	87	15	0

MARTIN SCHULTS, DR

To cash pd by Mr. Franklin	5	5	0
To a horse returned	8	0	0
Bal. due to M. S.	68	10	0
	£81	15	0

CR.

By waggon and team	43	10	0
By ditto's hire	35	5	0
By expenses	3	0	0
	81	15	0

ABRAHAM WHITEMAN. DR.

To cash pd by Mr. Franklin	5	5	0
To ditto pd by Mr. Scott	1	2	6
Balance	66	10	5
	72	17	11

CR.

By waggon and team	37	0	0
By hire on do	32	15	0
By expenses	3	2	11
	72	17	11

GEORGE MYERS, DR.

To cash pd by Mr. Franklin	5	5	0
To a horse returned	6	10	0
Bal. due	74	0	10
	85	15	10

CR.

By waggon and team	33	10	0
By do hire	38	5	0
By hire man and horse 53 days to Philada.	11	0	10
By expenses	3	0	0
	85	15	10

TETER OWLER, DR.

To cash pd by Mr. Frank.	.	5	5	0
To do pd by Mr. Scott	.	1	2	6
B.	.	61	16	6
		£68	4	0

CR.

By waggon and team	.	30	0	0
By hire ditto	.	35	9	0
By expenses	.	2	15	0
		68	4	0

MICHAEL KAMN, DR.

To cash pd by Mr. Franklin .	.	5	5	0
To a horse returned	.	8	0	0
Bal. due	.	65	13	6
		78	18	6

CR.

By waggon and team	.	40	0	0
By hire of ditto	.	35	18	6
By expenses, York	.	3	0	0
		78	18	6

JACOB HOOK, DR.

To cash pd by Mr. Frank. .	.	5	5	0
To do paid by Mr. McCloud	.		7	6
		80	5	0
		85	17	6

CR.

By waggon and team	.	42	10	0
By hire of ditto	.	40	7	6
By expenses, York	.	3	0	0
		85	17	6

William Bowsman, Dr.

To cash pd by Mr. Fr.	5	5	0
To do pd by Mr. Lake	20	0	0
To do pd by do	1	7	0
To 2 horses returned	25	0	0
To cash pd by Mr. Scott	1	2	6
Balance	80	18	5
	£133	12	11

Cr.

By waggon and team	71	0	0
By hire of ditto	59	5	0
By expenses	3	7	11
	133	12	11

February 10.
Philip Redrug, Dr.

To cash paid by Mr. Franklin	5	5	0
To do pd by Mr. McCloud		7	6
Bal. due to P. R.	80	12	6
	86	5	0

Cr.

By waggon and team	42	0	0
By hire of do	37	10	0
By man and horse overservice	3	15	0
By expenses	3	0	0
	86	5	0

Peter Gardner. Dr.

To cash pd by Mr. Franklin	5	5	0
To do pd by Mr. McCloud		7	6
To a horse returned	12	0	0
Bal. due to P. Gardner	76	6	0
	92	18	6

CR.

By waggon and team	.	.	.	.	47 10 0
By hire of ditto	.	.	.	.	37 10 0
By ditto more	.		.	.	4 18 6
By expenses (York)		.	.	.	3 0 0

£92 18 6

ROBERT CALLENDER, DR.

To cash pd by Mr. Leake	.	.	.	100 0 0
To do pd by do	.	.	.	21 12 0
To do pd	.	.	.	5 15 0
To do pd his drivers	.	.	.	11 12 6
To do pd by Mr. Scott	.	.	.	4 10 0
To 3 horses returned	:	.	.	24 0 0
Bal. due to R. C.	.	.	.	.1371 7 4

1538 16 10

CR.

By hire of 70 horses 41 days each			-	310 0 0
By 18 horses 31 days	.	.	.	55 16 0
By 6 horses 71 do	.	.	.	42 12 0
By 6 do 99 do	.	.	.	55 6 0
By hire 4 do	.	.	.	4 2 0
By hire of drivers	.	.	.	36 3 4
By 114 horses lost	.	.	.	.1043 17 6

1538 16 10

ROBER TAYLOR, DR.

To cash paid by Mr. Franklin	.	.	10 10 0
To do pd by Mr. Scott	.	.	2 5 0
To do pd by Mr. Lessly	.	.	7 0 0
Bal. due to Rob. Taylor	.	.	150 0 10

169 15 10

CR.

By 2 waggons and 8 horses lost	.				92	0	0
By 2 do &c. hire	.	.	38	5	0		
and	.	.	.	38	5	0		
				76	10	0		
Two horses failed, deduct	.	5	10	0		
					71	0	0
By expenses	.	.	.	·	.	6	15	10
					£169	15	10

MATHEW LAIRD DR.

To cash pd by Mr. F.	.	.	.	.	5	5	0
To do pd by Mr.	.	.	.	.	1	2	6
To do pd by Mr. Leake	.	.	.	1	7	0
Bal.	.	.	.	.	.	66	3	5
					73	17	11

CR.

By waggon and team lost	.	.	.	37	10	0
By hire of do	.	.	.	.	33	0	0
By expenses	.	.	.	.	3	7	11
					73	17	11

BARNARD HOLSINGER, DR.

To cash pd by Franklin	.	.	.	4	4	0
Bal. due to B. H.	.	.	.	.	54	0	0
					58	4	0

CR.

By 6 horses	.	.	.	.	.	27	0	0
To hire of do 52 days	.	.	.	31	4	0
					58	4	0

MICHAL TANNER, DR.

To cash paid by Mr. Fr.	5	5	0
To 3 horses returned	20	10	0
Bal. due to M. Tanner	52	5	4
	£78	0	4

CR.

By waggon and horse l.	40	0	0
By hire of do	26	5	0
By 1 horse 5 days hire 10s.			
1 do and 56 do 5.12	6	2	0
By hire of a driver	2	13	4
By expenses	3	0	0
	78	0	4

WILLIAM WILSON, DR.

To cash pd by Mr. F.	5	5	0
To do pd by Mr. Scott	1	2	6
	68	5	0
	74	12	6

CR.

By waggon and horses	39	10	0
By hire of ditto	32	2	6
By expenses	3	0	0
	74	12	6

WILLIAM SINCLAR, DR.

To cash pd by Mr. Franklin	4	4	0
To do pd by Mr. Scott		15	0
To do pd by Mr. Leake	1	7	0
Bal. due	52	15	10
	59	1	10

CR.

By 6 horses	.	.	.	.	.	29	17	6
By hire of ditto	.	.	.	.	.	20	16	0
By hire ot driver	.	.	.	.	.	5	8	4
By expenses	.	.	.	.	.	3	0	0
						£59	1	10

DANIEL LONG, DR.

To cash pd by Mr. Fr.	.	.	.	5	5	0
To do pd by Mr. S.	.	.	.	1	2	6
Bal.	. . . . . .	.	74	5	0
				80	12	6

CR.

By waggon and team	.	.	.	.	38	5	0
By hire ot do	.	.	.	.	39	7	6
By expenses, York	.	.	.	.	3	0	0
					80	12	6

THOMAS McCALL, DR.

To cash paid by Mr. Fr.	.	.	.	5	5	0
To do pd by Mr. Scott	.	.	.	.	1	2	6
To do pd by Mr. Lake	.	.	.	.	2	3	1½
Bal. due to T. M.	.	.	.	.	72	11	10½
				81	2	6

CR.

By waggon and team	.	.	.	.	46	0	0
By hire ot do	.	.	.	.	32	2	6
By expenses, York	.	.	.	.	3	0	0
					81	2	6

JOHN RICHMOND, DR.

								£	s	d
To cash pd by Mr. Fr.	.	.	.	.				5	5	0
To do pd by Mr. Scott	.	.	.	.				1	2	6
To do pd by Leake	.	.	5	5	0					
and	.	.	.	1	7	0				
								6	12	0
Bal. due to J. Richm'd	.	.	.					70	0	6
								£83	0	0

CR.

					£	s	d
By waggon and team	.	.	.	.	55	0	0
By hire of ditto	.	.	.	.	25	0	0
By expenses, York	.	.	.	.	3	0	0
					83	0	0

PETER BRILHEART, DR.

					£	s	d
To cash pd by Mr. F.	.	.	.	.	5	5	0
Bal.	.	.	.	.	.	68	5	0
					73	10	0

CR.

					£	s	d
By waggon and team	.	.	.	.	39	0	0
To hire of ditto	.	.	.	.	31	10	0
By expenses (York)	.	.	.	.	3	0	0
					73	10	0

JOHN TRICHLER, DR.

					£	s	d
To cash pd by Mr. F.	.	.	.	.	5	5	0
To do pd by Mr. Scott	.	.	.	.		7	6
Bal. due to J. T.	.	.	.	.	55	7	6
					61	0	0

CR.

					£	s	d
By waggon and team	.	.	.	.	32	0	0
By hire of do	.	.	.	.	26	0	0
By expenses, York	.	.	.	.	3	0	0
					61	0	0

DAVID WELCHHANOE, DR.

To cash pd by Mr. Franklin	.	.	5	5	0
			83	15	0
			£89	0	0

CR.

By waggon and team	.	.	.	.	43	10	0
By hire of do	.	.	.	.	42	10	0
By expenses (York)	.	.	.	.	3	0	0
					89	0	0

LODWICK SOLOMON MILLER, DR.

To cash pd by Mr. F.	.	.	.	.	5	5	0
Bal.	.	.	.	.	.	79	2	6
					84	7	6

CR.

By waggon and team	.	.	.·	.	44	10	0
By hire of ditto	.	.	.	.	36	17	6
By expenses, York	.	.	.	3	0	0
					84	7	6

JOHN SMITH, DR.

To cash pd by Mr. Fr.	.	.	.	.	5	5	0
To do paid by Scott	.	.	.	.	1	2	6
To bal.	.	.	.	.	.	84	17	6
					91	5	0

CR.

By waggon and team	.	.	.	.	50	0	0
By waggon hire	.	.	.	.	38	5	0
By expenses	.	.	.	.	.	3	0	0
					91	5	0

PETER CAKLAR, DR.

		£	s	d
To cash paid by Mr. Frauklin	. .	3	3	0
To do pd by Mr. Lake			15	0
Bal. due to P. Caklar	. . .	49	13	8
		£53	11	8

CR.

		£	s	d
By 6 horses	.	22	0	0
By hire of 5 horses	. . .	24	10	0
By driver 49 days	. . . .	4	1	8
By expenses	.	3	0	0
		53	11	8

ANTHONY SELL, DR.

		£	s	d
To cash pd by Mr. Franklin	. .	5	5	0
To do pd by Mr. Scott . . .	.	1	2	6
Bal. due to A. S. . . .	.	70	7	6
		76	15	0

CR.

		£	s	d
By waggon and team	. . . .	35	10	0
By hire of ditto .	. . . .	38	5	0
By expenses, (York)	. . .	3	0	0
		76	15	0

JACOB HAMMON, DR.

		£	s	d
To cash paid by Mr. Fr.	. .	5	5	0
Bal. due to J. H. . . .	.	63	5	0
		68	10	0

CR.

		£	s	d
By waggon and team	. . . .	29	10	0
By waggon hire .	. . .	36	0	0
By expenses	. . .	3	0	0
		£68	10	0

JOHN FRANKLBARBER, DR.

		£	s	d
To cash pd by Mr. Fr.	. . .	5	5	0
To do pd by Mr. Scott	. . . .	1	2	6
Bal. due to J. F.	. . . .	62	12	6
		£69	0	0

CR.

		£	s	d
By waggon and team	. . . .	41	10	0
By waggon hire	. . . . .	24	10	0
By expenses	. . . . . .	3	0	0
		69	0	0

HENRY JACOBS, DR.

		£	s	d
To cash pd by Mr. Franklin	. .	5	5	0
Bal. due to H. J.	. . . .	67	7	0
		72	12	0

CR.

		£	s	d
By waggou and team	. . . .	35	15	0
By waggon hire	. . . . .	33	17	0
By expenses	. . . . . .	3	0	0
		72	12	0

HARBANUS ASHEBRINER, DR

		£	s	d
To cash pd by Mr. Franklin	. .	5	5	0
Balance due to H. A.	. . .	81	17	0
		87	2	6

CR.

		£	s	d
By waggon and team	. . . .	44	0	0
By waggon hire	. . . . .	40	2	6
By expenses	. . . . . .	3	0	0
		87	2	6

THOMAS KINTON, DR.

		£	s	d
To cash pd by Mr. Scott	. . .		15	0
To do paid by Mr. Lake	. . .	1	7	0
Bal. due to Thos. Kinton	. . .	132	2	0
		£134	4	0

CR.

		£	s	d
By 11 horses lost	.	110	0	0
By hire of ditto	.	24	4	0
		134	4	0

PETER LEMON, DR.

		£	s	d
To cash pd by Mr. F.	. . .		4	4	0
To ditto pd by Mr. Scott	. .		15	0
To 3 horses driver ran off with	.	17	5	0
Bal. due	.	31	10	4
		53	14	4

CR.

		£	s	d
By 6 horses	.	31	7	0
By hire of ditto	.	20	14	0
By driver's hire 20 days at 20d.	.	1	13	4
		53	14	4

RUDOLF LITTLE PETER, DR

		£	s	d
To cash pd by Mr. F.	. . .	5	5	0
To do pd by Mr. McCloud	. .		15	0
Bal.	.	73	0	0
		79	0	0

CR.

		£	s	d
By waggon and team	. . .	38	10	0
By hire of ditto	.	37	10	0
By expenses	.	3	0	0
		79	0	0

GEORGE MICHAEL STOVER, DR.

	£	s	d
To cash pd by Mr. Franklin . .	5	5	0
To a horse returned	9	0	0
Bal. due	68	15	0
	£83	0	0

CR.

	£	s	d
By waggon and team	40	0	0
By hire of ditto	40	0	0
By expenses (York)	3	0	0
	83	0	0

CHRISTOPHER DIELINHEFER, DR.

	£	s	d
To cash pd by Mr. F.	5	5	0
To ditto pd by Mr. Scott . . .	1	2	6
Balance	56	10	0
	62	17	6

CR.

	£	s	d
By waggon and team lost . . .	30	10	0
By hire of ditto	29	7	6
By expenses, York	3	0	0
	62	17	6

ADAM CRAIMER, DR.

	£	s	d
To cash pd by Mr. F.	4	4	0
Bal. due to A. C.	63	15	8
	67	19	8
To a horse returned	5	0	0
To hire of a horse	4	18	0
Bal. due to A. Craimer . . .	53	17	8
	63	15	8

Cr.

By 6 horses	31	10	0
By hire of ditto	29	8	0
By hire of a driver	4	1	8
By expenses (Yerk)	3	0	0
	£67	19	8
By balance above	63	15	8

Christian Stoder, Dr.

Due to C. Stoder		15	0

Cr.

By the hire of a waggon for 1 day .		15	0

February 11th.

Michael Charles, Dr.

To cash pd by Mr. Franklin . .	5	5	0
	72	16	0
	78	1	0

Cr.

By waggon and team lost . . .	44	5	0
By hire of ditto	30	16	0
By expenses	3	0	0
	78	1	0

John Kinkade, Dr.

Due to John K.	5	6	0

Cr.

By 31 horses hired . . .	5	6	0

John McCord, Dr.

To cash pd by Mr. Fr.	5	5	0
To do pd by Mr. Leake . . .	2	14	0
Bal. due to J. M.	95	6	0
	103	5	0

Cr.

By waggon and team lost . . .	60	0	0
By waggon hire	38	5	0
By travelling expenses by contract .	5	0	0
	£103	5	0

JOSHUA DRUMMOND, DR.

Due to J. D.	67	8	4

Cr.

By 6 horses lost	42	0	0
By hire of ditto	21	0	0
By the hire of driver	1	8	4
By expenses . , ...	3	0	0
	67	8	4

CHRISTIAN LOW, DR.

To cash pd by Mr. Fr.	5	5	0
To error having been so much over credited	2	2	6
	78	10	0
	85	17	6

Cr.

By waggon and team lost . . .	37	10	0
By waggon hire	45	7	6
By expenses (York)	3	0	0
	85	17	6

PETER SHULTZ, DR.

To Benja. Franklin cash . . .	5	5	0
To 2 horses returned . . .	18	0	0
	69	0	0
	92	5	0

CR.

By waggon and team.	.	.	.	.	47	10	0
By hire of ditto	.	.	.	.	41	15	0
By expenses (York)	.	.	.	.	3	0	0
				£92	5	0

ABRAHAM SELL, DR.

To cash pd by Mr. Fr.	.	.	.	.	10	10	0
To do pd byMr. Scott	.	.	.	.	2	5	0
Bal.	.	.	.	.	.	150	8	0
				163	3	0

CR.

By 2 waggons and team	.	.	.	84	5	0
By hire 2 waggons, &c.	.	.	.	72	18	0
By expenses (York)	.	.	.	6	0	0
			163	3	0

NICHOLAS CLAY, DR.

To cash pd by Mr. Fr.	.	.	.	.	5	5	0
Bal.	.	.	.	.	.	83	2	6
				88	7	6

CR.

By waggon and team	.	.	.	.	45	10	0
By hire of ditto	.	.	.	.	39	17	6
By expenses, York	.	.	.	3	0	0
				88	7	6

JOHN DUFFIELD, DR.

To cash pd by Mr. Fr.	.	.	.	.	5	5	0
To do pd by Mr. Scott	.	.	.	.	1	2	6
B.	.	.	.	.	.	71	15	0
				78	2	6

CR.

By waggon and team	.	.	46	10	0
By hire of ditto	.	.	28	12	6
By expenses (York)	.	.	3	0	0
		£78	2	6

PHILIP HAINS, DR.

To cash pd by Mr. Fr.	.	.	4	4	0
To do pd by Mr. Scott	.	.		15	0
Bal.	.	.	56	1	8
		61	0	8

CR.

By 6 horses	.	.	22	10	0
By hire of ditto 52 days 2s.	.	.	31	4	0
By expenses	.	.	3	0	0
By driver 52 days at 20d.	.	.	4	6	8
		61	0	8

JOHN BUOKANAN, DR.

To cash pd by Mr. F.	.	.	5	5	0
To do pd by Mr. Scott	.	.	6	7	6
Cash of Mr. Lake	.	.	1	7	0
Bal. due to J. B.	.	.	87	10	6
		100	10	0

CR.

By waggon and team lost	.	.	49	0	0
By hire of do	.	.	48	10	0
By expenses (York)	.	.	3	0	0
		100	10	0

ROBERT McPHERSON, DR.

To cash pd by Mr. F.	.	.	5	5	0
To do pd by Mr. Leake	.	.	2	14	0
To do pd by Mr. Scott	.	.	1	10	0
To 2 horses returned	.	.	13	0	0
Balance due to R. M	.	.	90	5	6
		112	14	6

CR.

By waggon and team lost . . .	47	10	0
By hire of do	62	4	6
By expenses (York)	3	0	0
	£112	14	6

ALEXANDER BROWN, DR.

To cash pd by Mr. Franklin . . .	5	5	0
To do pd by Mr. Scott . . .	1	2	6
To do pd by Mr. Leake . . .	5	5	0
Bal.	92	2	6
	103	15	0

CR.

By waggon and team lost . . .	48	10	0
By waggon hire, &c	52	5	0
By expenses	3	0	0
	103	15	0

MICHAEL BARD, DR.

To cash pd by Mr. Franklin . . .	5	5	0
Bal. due to M. B.	68	10	0
	73	15	0

CR.

By waggon and team lost . . .	34	0	0
By hire of ditto	36	15	0
By expenses, York	3	0	0
	73	15	0

CHARLES HAMILTON, DR.

To cash pd by Mr. F.	4	4	0
	55	14	0
	59	18	0

CR.

By 6 horses lost	.	27	10	0
By hire of ditto 49 days 2s.	. .	29	8	0
By expenses (York) . . .	.	3	0	0
		£59	18	0

LEONARD EMBLE, DR.

To cash paid by Mr. Franklin	. .	5	5	0
Bal. due to L. E. . . .	.	86	7	6
		91	12	6

CR.

By waggon and team lost	. . .	49	0	0
By waggon hire . . .	. .	39	12	6
By expenses (York) . . .	.	3	0	0
		91	12	6

WILLIAM DUFFIELD, DR.

To cash pd by Mr. F. . .	. .	5	5	0
To ditto pd by Mr. Scott	. . .	1	2	6
Bal. due to W. D. . . .	.	64	15	0
		71	2	6

CR.

By waggon and team lost	. . .	40	10	0
By hire of ditto . . .	. .	27	12	6
By expenses (YORK) . . .	.	3	0	0
		71	2	6

CONRAD KENSEL, DR.

To cash pd by Mr. F. . .	. .	5	5	0
Bal. due to C. K. . . .	.	71	17	6
		77	2	6

CR.

By waggon and team lost	.	.	. 31	0	0
By hire of do, &c	.	.	. 43	2	6
By expenses (York)	.	.	. 3	0	0

	£77	2	6

JACOB MILLER, DR.

To cash pd by Mr. F.	. . . 4	4	0
To a horse returned	. . . 7	0	0
Bal. due to J. Miller	. . . 63	4	0

	74	8	0

CR.

By 6 horses	 40	0	0
By hire of do	 29	8	0
By hire of the driver	. . . 2	0	0
By expenses (York)	. . . 3	0	0

	74	8	0

HENRY BUTT, DR.

To cash pd by Mr. F.	. . . 5	5	0
To do pd by Mr. Scott	. . . 1	2	6
Bal. due to	 67	15	0

	74	2	6

CR.

By waggon and team lost	. . . 29	0	0
By hire of ditto	 42	2	6
By expenses, York)	. . . 3	0	0

	74	2	6

JACOB WERTZ, DR.

To cash pd by Mr. F.	. . . 5	5	0
To do pd by Mr. Scott	. . 1	2	6
	64	15	0

	71	2	6

CR.

By waggon and team	.	.	.	.	31	0	0
By hire of ditto	.	.	.	.	37	2	6
By expenses (York)	.	.	.	.	3	0	0

£71   2   6

TITTER MYER, DR.

To cash pd by Mr. Fr.	.	.	.	5	5	0
Bal. due to T. M.	.	.	.	63	12	6

68   17   6

CR.

By waggon and team	.	.	.	.	31	0	0
By hire of ditto	.	.	.	.	34	17	6
By expenses	.	.	.	.	3	0	0

68   17   6

JOHN GOOD, DR.

To cash pd by Mr. F.	.	.	.	.	5	5	0
To do pd by Scott	.	.	.	.	1	2	6
					101	17	6

108   5   0

CR.

By waggon and team	.	.	.	.	67	0	0
By hire of ditto	.	.	.	.	38	5	0
By expenses	.	.	.	.	3	0	0

108   5   0

PHILIP FURNAY. DR.

To cash pd by Mr. F.	.	.	.	5	5	0
To do pd by Mr. Scott	.	.	.	1	2	6
Bal.	.	.	.	.	.	70	19	6

77   7   0

CR.

By waggon and team	42	0	0
By hire of ditto	32	7	0
By expenses (York)	3	0	0
	£77	7	0

MICHAEL TASSE, DR.

To cash paid by Mr. Frank. . .	35	0	0
To ditto paid by Mr. Leake . .	38	2	0
To ditto pd by Mr. Scott . . .	1	10	0
Balance due to M. T. . . .	154	4	0
	228	16	0

CR.

By 15 horses lost	136	10	0
By hire of men and horses . .	56	4	0
By travelling expenses . . .	12	12	0
By hire of horses	5	10	0
By 3 horses lost	18	0	0
	228	16	0

JAMES HALL, DR.

To cash paid by Mr. F. . . .	5	5	0
To ditto paid by Mr. Scott . .	1	2	6
To do pd by Mr. Leake . .		7	6
Bal. due to J. H. . . .	68	18	4
	75	13	4

CR.

By waggon and team lost . . .	45	10	0
By hire of ditto	27	3	4
By travelling expenses	3	0	0
	75	13	4

ARTHUR FORSTER, DR.

To cash paid by Mr. F.	5	5	0
To do paid by Mr. Scott	16	6	3
To do paid by Mr. Lake	1	7	0
To a horse returned	9	0	0
Bal. due to A. F.	61	13	5
	£93	11	8

CR.

By waggon and team lost	45	0	0
By hire of ditto	45	11	8
By expenses	3	0	0
	93	11	8

JOSEPH DAVIS DR.

To cash pd by Mr. F.	5	5	0
To ditto pd him by Scott	1	2	6
To ditto pd by Mr. Lake	13	18	0
Bal. due to J. D.	72	14	6
	93	0	0

CR.

By waggon and team lost	50	0	0
By waggon hire	35	5	0
By the hire of a horse	4	15	0
By expenses	3	0	0
	93	0	0

JAMES MATHEWS, DR.

To cash paid by Mr. F.	5	5	0
To ditto paid by Mr. Scott	1	2	6
To ditto paid by Mr. Leake	2	14	0
Bal. due to J. M.	66	18	6
	76	0	0

CR.

By wagon and team . . .	37	0	0
By hire of ditto	36	0	0
By expenses	3	0	0
	£76	0	0

DAVID MURREY, DR.

To cash paid by Mr. F. . . .	2	2	0
Bal. due to D. M.	27	18	4
	30	0	4

CR.

By 3 horses lost	16	10	0
To hire of 3 horses 14 days . .	4	4	0
By ditto 3 do . . .	3	8	0
By hire of a driver . . .	4	8	4
By expenses	1	10	0
	30	0	4

JAMES FOLEY, DR.

Due to J. F.	18	0	0

CR.

By one horse lost . . .	8	0	0
By another horse lost . . .	8	0	0
By his own services . . .	2	0	0
	18	0	0

JOHN WRIGHT, DR.

Due to John Wright . . .	13	18	0

CR.

To hire and loss of a horse . .	13	18	0

DR. ADAM SIMON KYHN, DR.

To cash pd by Mr. Franklin . .	5	5	0
Bal. due to A. S. K. . .	103	7	11
	108	12	11

CR.

By waggon and team lost . . .	67	0	0
By hire of ditto	38	5	0
By expenses . - . . .	3	7	11

£108 12 11

LUDWIG SHRIVER, DR.

To cash pd by Mr. F.	5	5	0
To ditto paid by Mr. Scott . . .	1	2	6
To 2 horses returned	23	0	0
Bal. due to L. S.	87	7	6

116 15 0

CR.

By waggon and team lost . . .	55	0	0
By hire of ditto	58	15	0
By expenses	3	0	0

116 15 0

JACOB HAULDIMAN & COMPY., DR.

Due	3	17	6

CR

By hire of 31 horses 1 day at 2s. 6d. per diem	3	17	6

JAMES HAMILTON, DR.

To cash pd by Mr. Leake . . .	2	3	3
Bal. due to J. H.	2	16	9

5 0 0

CR.

By hire of himself 2 mos. . .	5	0	0

RICHARD LONG, Dr.

To cash paid by Mr. Frank. . .	5	5	0
To ditto paid by Mr. Scott . .	1	2	6
To ditto by Mr. Leake . . .	2	14	0
Bal due to R. L. . . .	94	1	10

103 3 4

CR.

By waggon and horses lost . .	66	0	0
By waggon hire	34	3	4
By expenses	3	0	0
	£103	3	4

JAMES LONG, DR.

To cash pd by Mr. F. . . .	5	5	0
To do paid by Mr. Scott . . .	1	2	6
To do paid by Mr. Leake . . .	2	14	0
To a horse returned	9	0	0
Balance due to J. L. . . .	79	17	8
	97	19	2

CR.

By waggon and team	55	0	0
By hire of ditto	39	19	2
By expenses	3	0	0
	97	19	2

BENJAMIN BLYTHE, DR.

To cash pd by Mr. F. . . .	5	5	0
To do pd by Mr. Scott	1	2	6
To do paid by Mr. Leake . . .	1	7	0
To a horse returned . . .	10	0	0
Balance due to Benjamin Blythe .	93	0	6
	110	15	0

CR.

By waggon and team	56	0	0
By hire of ditto	51	15	0
By expenses	3	0	0
	110	15	0

BARNABAS HUGHES, OF SHIPPENSBURG, DR.

To cash paid by Mr. Leake . . .		14	0
Balance due to B. N. . . .	16	18	0
	17	12	0

CR.

By 2 horses lost	8	16	0
By the hire of the said horses 44 days at 2s. each	8	16	0
	17	12	0

JOHN THOMPSON, DR.

To cash pd by Mr. Franklin . .	5	5	0
To do paid by Mr. Scott . . .	1	2	6
To do pd by Mr. Lake . . .	1	8	0
Bal.	73	9	6
	81	5	0

CR.

By waggon and team lost . .	40	0	0
By hire of ditto	38	5	0
By expenses	3	0	0
	81	5	0

THEOBALD SHALLAS, DR.

To cash pd by Mr. Fr.	5	5	0
Bal. due to T. S.	64	10	0
	69	15	0

CR.

By waggon	38	10	0
By hire of ditto . . .	28	5	0
By expenses	3	0	0
	69	15	0

JOHN BRUBBAKER DR.

To cash pd	3	3	0
Bal. due to Jno. B. . . .	5	7	9
	8	7	9

CR.

By pasturage of 148 horses	.	. £8	7	9

JACOB HUNSINGER, DR.

To cash pd by Mr. F.	.	.	.	.	. 5	5	0
To do pd by Scott	.	.	.	.	1	2	6
Balance due to J. H.	.	.	.	67	8	0

		73	15	6

CR.

By waggon	.	.	.	.	.	. 38	10	0
By hire of ditto	.	.	.	.	. 32	5	6
By expenses	.	.	.	.	.	3	0	0

		73	15	6

THOMAS GIBBS, DR.

To cash pd by	.	.	.	.	. 5	5	0
To do paid by Mr. Scott	.	.	. 1	2	6
To do paid by Mr. Leake	.	.	. 1	7	0
Bal. due to T. G.	.	.	.	. 96	2	2

		103	16	8

CR.

By waggon and team lost	.	.	. 53	0	0
By hire of ditto	.	.	.	. 37	15	0
By expenses	.	.	.	.	. 3	0	0
By hire of horses and driver to Phila.	. 10	1	8

		103	16	8

JOSEPH MCKINNY, DR.

To cash paid by Mr. F.	.	.	. 5	5	0
To do pd by Mr. Scott	.	.	. 1	2	6
To do pd by Mr. Leake	.	.	. 1	7	0
By 2 horses returned	.	.	.	. 15	10	0
Bal. due	.	-	.	.	.	. 79	10	6

		102	15	0

CR.

	£	s.	d.
By waggon and team	34	0	0
By hire of ditto	65	15	0
By expenses	3	0	0
	£102	15	0

JOHN WAGGONER, DR.

		£	s.	d.
To cash pd by Mr. F. . . .		5	5	0
Bal. due to J. Waggoner . .		59	3	6
		64	8	6

CR.

	£	s.	d.
By waggon and team lost . . .	32	15	0
By hire of ditto	28	13	6
By expenses	3	0	0
	64	8	6

JOHN McCOMBE, DR.

	£	s.	d.
To cash pd by Adam Hoops . . .	1	8	0
To a horse returned	3	0	0
Bal. due to J. M.	9	10	0
	13	18	0

CR.

	£	s.	d.
By 2 horses lost	8	0	0
By hire of ditto	4	18	0
By expenses at 10s. a horse . . .	1	0	0
	13	18	0

ABRAHAM ERVIN, DR.

	£	s.	d.
To cash paid by Mr. F. . . .	5	5	0
Bal. due to A. E.	90	0	0
	95	5	0

CR.

By waggon and team	.	.	.	.	54	0	0
By hire ot ditto	.	.	.	.	38	5	0
By expenses	.	.	.	.	3	0	0
					£95	5	0

JOHN REYNOLDS, DR.

To cash paid by Mr. Hoops	.	.	2	16	0
			48	0	0
			50	16	0

CR.

By 4 horses lost	.	.	.	.	28	0	0
By hire of horses	.	.	.	.	20	16	0
By expenses	.	.	.	.	.	2	0	0
					50	16	0

THOMAS CHRISTIE, DR

To cash pd by Mr. Lake	.	.	.	2	14	0
Bal. due to T. C.	.	.	.	.	13	7	0
					16	1	0

CR.

By hire of a horse	.	.	.	.	4	4	0
By do mare	.	.	.	.	5	12	0
By do of a driver	.	.	.	.	6	5	0
					16	1	0

MOSES STUART, DR.

To cash pd by Mr. Scott	.	.	.		15	0
To do pd by Mr. Hoops	.	.	.		7	6
Bal. due to M. S.	.	.	.	.	50	13	10
					51	16	4

CR.

By 4 horses at £8	.	.	.	.	32	0	0
By hire of ditto	.	.	.	.	16	8	0
By do of the driver	.	.	.	.	3	8	4
					51	16	4

JAMES MORRISON. DR.

To cash pd by Mr. Scott	1	10	0
To do pd by Mr. Leake	2	14	0
Bal. due to J. M.	33	8	8
	£37	12	8

CR.

By 2 horses lost	17	0	0
To hire of ditto	9	16	0
By do of 2 drivers	10	16	8
	37	12	8

BENJAMIN PRICE, DR.

Vide B. Price's first account settled page 1

Due to B. Price	137	7	4

CR.

By the bal. of his first acct. page	109	17	4
By 4 horses lost at £7	28	0	0
	137	17	4

ADAM HOOPES, DR.

Due to A. H.	5	4	0

CR.

By hire of 26 horse 2 days	5	4	0

JOHN MYERS, DR.

To cash paid by Mr. Fr.	5	5	0
Bal. due to J. M.	85	10	0
	90	15	0

CR.

By a waggon and team	45	0	0
By hire of ditto	42	10	0
By expenses	3	0	0
	90	10	0

INDEX.

La Fievre, Daniel 13
La Fievre, Samuel 12
Laird, Mathew 48
Lander, Fred. 27
Landess, Benjamin 16
Lauman, Bernard 38
Lawrey, Daniel 18
Lawrey, James 21
Lemon, Peter 55
Liphart, Henry 43
Lippart, Hans Adam 32
Little, George 28
Lock, Peter 7
Long, Daniel 50
Long, James 69
Long, Richard 68
Low, Christian 58

McCall, Thomas 50
McCombe, John 72
McCord, John 57
McKinny, Joseph 71
McPherson, Robert 60
Magee, Richard 27
Mathews, James 66
Miller, Jacob 63
Miller, John 21
Miller, Ludwig Solomon 52
Mitchell, Thomas 28
Moore, John 22
Morrison, James . . . . . , 74
Mummoia, Jacob 18
Murrey, David 67
Myer, Titter 64
Myer, Vincent 20
Myers, George 44
Myers, George Ernst 37
Myers, John . . , ... 74

Stoder, Christian 57
Stout, David 42
Stover, George Michael 56
Stuart, Moses 73
Swaine, Caleb, for Bishop 12

Tanner, Michal 49
Tasse, Michael 65
Taylor, Robert . . . . . . • 47
Thompson, John 70
Tread, Peter 89
Trichler, John 51

Upright, Philip 31

Waggoner, John . • . . . ∵ 72
Walbone, Christian . . ∶ . 27-36-37
Welch, John 11
Welchhance, Jacob David 52
Welchouer, Jacob 41
Wertz, Jacob 63
Whiteman, Abraham ∶ 44
Whiteman, Martin 17
Wilkyns, William 25
Willhiem, Jacob 15
Wilson, William 49
Worley, Caleb 13
Worley, Francis 38
Wright, John 67

www.ingramcontent.com/pod-product-compliance
Lightning Source LLC
Chambersburg PA
CBHW022141090426
42742CB00010B/1345